Making Graphs

Bar Graphs

by Vijaya Khisty Bodach

Capstone press

Mankato, Minnesota

A+ Books are published by Capstone Press,
151 Good Counsel Drive, P.O. Box 669, Mankato, Minnesota 56002.
www.capstonepress.com

1 2 3 4 5 6 12 11 10 09 08 07

Library of Congress Cataloging-in-Publication Data
Bodach, Vijaya.
  Bar graphs / by Vijaya Khisty Bodach.
    p. cm. — (A+ books. Making graphs)
  Includes bibliographical references and index.
  ISBN-13: 978-1-4296-0040-8
  ISBN-10: 1-4296-0040-3
  1. Mathematics—Graphic methods—Juvenile literature. I. Title. II. Series.
QA40.5.B64 2007
510—dc22   2007004670

Summary: Uses simple text and photographs to describe making and using bar graphs.

Credits
Heather Adamson, editor; Juliette Peters, designer; Wanda Winch, photo researcher;
Kelly Garvin, photo stylist

Photo Credits
All photos Capstone Press/Karon Dubke

Note to Parents, Teachers, and Librarians
Making Graphs uses color photographs and a nonfiction format to introduce readers to graphing
concepts. *Bar Graphs* is designed to be read aloud to a pre-reader, or to be read independently
by an early reader. Images and activities encourage mathematical thinking in early readers
and listeners. The book encourages further learning by including the following sections: Table
of Contents, Glossary, Read More, Internet Sites, and Index. Early readers may need assistance
using these features.

Table of Contents

Zebras, elephants, and giraffes.
Let's play with the animals in the toy room.
How many of each kind do we have?

We can sort the animals into groups.
Which group has the most?

Let's put the animals in rows by kind.
Now we can see the zebra group
has the most.

We have made a
bar graph. Bar graphs
compare the amount
of each kind.

We can compare animals
without lining them up.
Let's use paper to make a graph.

Put the names of the animals
on the bottom.
Numbers go along the side.

We have four giraffes. One, two, three, four. Fill the bar up to four.

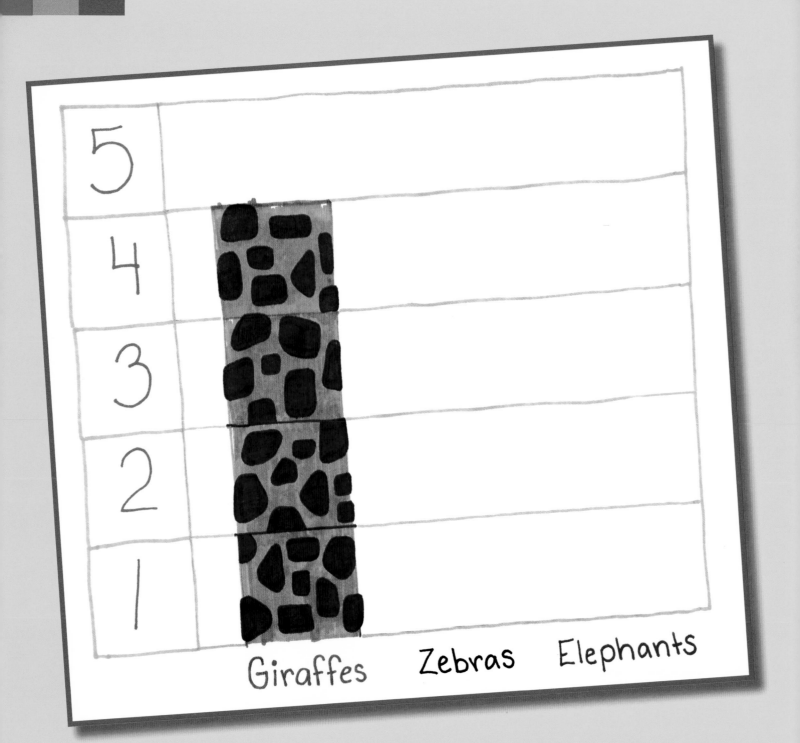

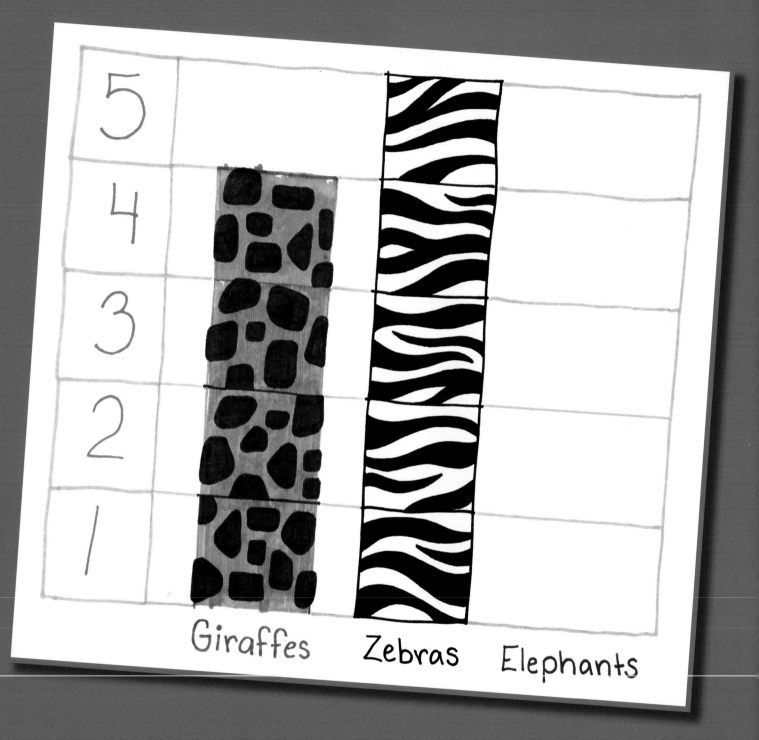

Color the zebra bar up to five. One, two, three, four, five.

Don't forget our two elephants.

The taller the bar,
the more of something we have.
Our bar graph shows we have
the most zebras.

Bar graphs can go up and down,
or from side to side.
This is the same information on its side.
It looks a lot like the rows of toys.

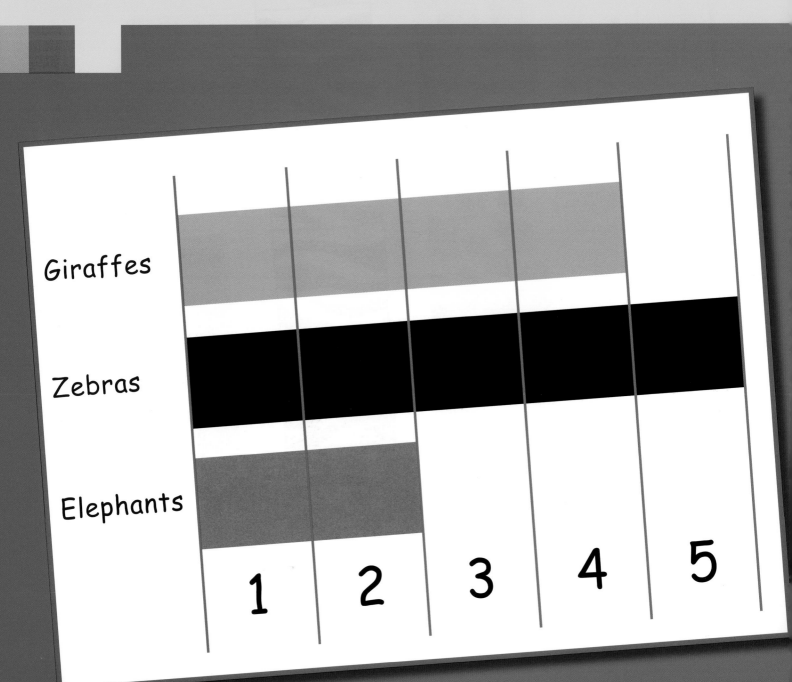

Did we buy more apples, oranges, or bananas at the market?

Let's make a graph
and compare.

Bananas

Apples

Oranges

1 2 3 4 5

Let's write the name of the fruit on the side.
The numbers can go along the bottom.

19

We have the fewest bananas.
The yellow bar for bananas is the shortest.

We have the most oranges.
The orange bar is the longest.

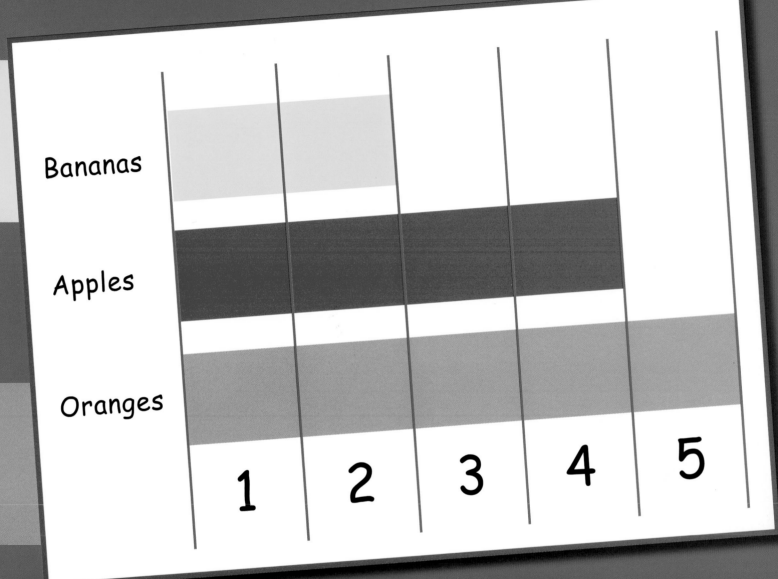

Bananas

Apples

Oranges

1 2 3 4 5

A group of friends gives us lots to graph.
Each kid has worn a favorite color shirt.

Blue is the most popular color.
Only one child likes yellow best.

We can make a graph of hair color.
Which color is the most common?

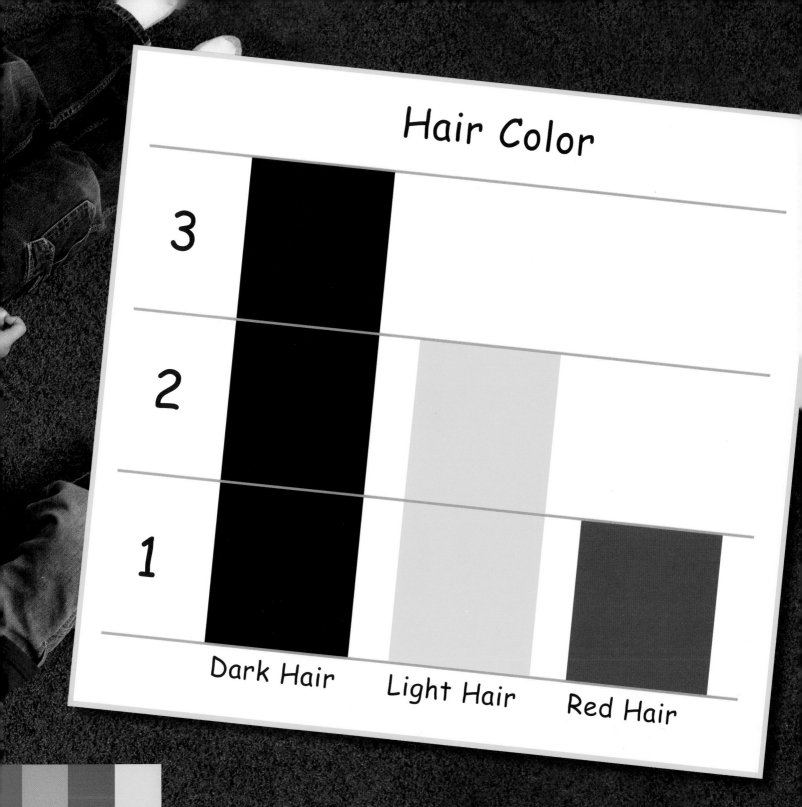

Hair Color

3			
2			
1			
	Dark Hair	Light Hair	Red Hair

Dark hair is the most common.
Light hair is less common.
Red hair is the least common.

Cats are more popular than dogs
with these kids. One child has no pets.

How would you graph these foods?
Your graph will look different if you sort
by color, type of food, or the first letter
of its name.

Glossary

bar (BAR)—a long, flat, block shape; on a graph, the taller or longer the bar, the more of something you have.

compare (kuhm-PARE)—to judge one thing against another

graph (GRAF)—to use a picture that compares numbers or amounts; graphs use bars, lines, or parts of a circle to compare.

row (ROH)—a line of things put side by side

sort (SORT)—to separate things into groups

Read More

Bader, Bonnie. *Graphs.* All Aboard Reading. Station Stop 2. New York: Grosset & Dunlap, 2003.

Leedy, Loreen. *The Great Graph Contest.* New York: Holiday House, 2005.

Internet Sites

FactHound offers a safe, fun way to find Internet sites related to this book. All of the sites on FactHound have been researched by our staff.

Here's how:

1. Visit *www.facthound.com*

2. Choose your grade level.

3. Type in this book ID **1429600403** for age-appropriate sites. You may also browse subjects by clicking on letters, or by clicking on pictures and words.

4. Click on the **Fetch It** button.

FactHound will fetch the best sites for you!

Index